CHRONICLES OF LIGHT & AIR

Other Books by Denham Grierson
published by Coventry Press

Turning in Time
Sharing Water by the River
Music From a Breaking Wave

> The form of things unknown, the poet's pen
> Turns them to shapes, and gives to airy nothing
> A local habitation and a name.

(A Midsummer Night's Dream, Act 5)

POEMS FOR
A TIME OF HEAVINESS

CHRONICLES OF LIGHT & AIR

DENHAM GRIERSON

COVENTRY PRESS

Published in Australia by
Coventry Press
33 Scoresby Road
Bayswater VIC 3153

ISBN 9781922589217

Copyright © Denham Grierson 2022

All rights reserved. Other than for the purposes and subject to the conditions prescribed under the *Copyright Act*, no part of this publication may be reproduced, stored in a retrieval system, or transmitted in any form or by any means, electronic, mechanical, photocopying, recording or otherwise, without the prior permission of the publisher.

Catalogue-in-Publication entry is available from the National Library of Australia
http://catalogue.nla.gov.au

Cover design by Ian James – www.jgd.com.au
Text design by Coventry Press
Set in Fontin

Printed in Australia

Contents

Foreword 11
Introduction 14
Acknowledgments 16

Light 17

    Thoughts of light and air 18
    A letter to my grandsons 19
    Song 20
    Skinned 21
    Warren 22
    Supermarket 24
    Fading 25
    A conversation with Rilke 26
    Jazz in time 27
    First people 28
    Treasure 29
    Confession in a time of self-isolation 30
    Criticism 30
    Tomorrow 31
    Isolation 32
    Coming 33
    Morning 33
    Timing is everything 34
    Guardians 35
    University of the Third Age 36
    Juggler 36
    Mother 37
    Letting go 38
    The colour of the wind 39

Clive James	40
Bells	40
Status	41
Morning walk	42
Parable	44
Perspective	45
Where or when	46
Child	47
Voice	48
Here and there	49
Magician	50
Phone call	51
Another time, another place	52
Listen	53
Tide	54
Abandonment	55
Let it go	55
Measure	56
Rain	57
Crepe-Myrtle	57
Knowledge	58
Grasshoppers	58
Hard rubbish pick up	59
Wetlands	60
Shadow	60
Moments	61
Waking in fright	62
Once upon a time	63
Today	64
West wind	65
Impression	66
Apple tree	67
Scarring	68
Looking glance	69

Intermission 71

    Wetland 72
    Tap dance 75
    Wetland reprise 76

Air 79

    Lesson 80
    Shining 81
    The season of plague 82
    A life imagined 83
    Deconstruction 84
    From far away 85
    Unnameable 86
    Tree 87
    Sacred space 88
    Incense 89
    Dance master 90
    A response to Martin Heidegger in his words 91
    Reflection 92
    Cost 92
    Funeral 93
    Weathervane 94
    Wattle tree 95
    Colouring book 96
    Design 97
    Telling of angels 98
    Beginnings 98
    All together now 100
    Yellow 101
    Faith 101
    God consciousness 102
    Good Friday 103
    Resurrection Monday 104
    Bowling green 104
    Dover Beach revisited 106

Spirit	106
Buddha in the garden	107
Denouemont	108
Descent	108
Yearning	109
Brainstorm	110
Garden	111
Vergangenheitsaufarbeitung	112
Day's end	113
Kingdom	113
Fullness	114
Seminar	115
Speechless	116
Wordless	117
Progress	118
Poetic task	119
Holy	120
Letter	121
Apparition	121
White board	122
Turning over	123
A new tomorrow	124
Understanding	125
Necessity	126
Forever	126
Conversations of the living	128
The God event	129
Physics	130
Sovereignty	131
Are you ready for fire?	132
A new creation	133
End	134

Foreword

Good theology and poetry have gone hand in hand for literally thousands of years. Great poetry has been handed down in musical settings as some of our most beloved hymns. Many of the Psalms in the Hebrew Bible were originally sung as statements of faith. Story/songs have been used for ages to capture young minds with the basics of teaching about faith, faith communities, and our life meanings.

If, as Emerson said, 'The earth laughs in flowers', then surely it smiles in verse. And with these, as in so many of Denham's hundreds of verses, we must smile at ourselves as the familiar becomes profound, the ordinary awakes, and old truths give birth to new awareness.

We are, in fact, living in a time of 'heaviness'. Ancient bitter conflicts seem to come full circle, pandemics bring to light human indifference and social disparities, and civility seems like a dream from a distant past. We could recite a thousand times over the conflicts that have been plagued by human greed and prejudice for millennia. But that would not add a glimmer of light or a breath of fresh air to our stale dreams. We need to take a fresh look at what is the common good and breathe hope once more into it. Denham leads us in this direction. New understandings of old certainties? Yes. Fresh intellectual fashions and unthought actions? Yes. Shed doctrines and new beauties? Absolutely! From isolation to carrying the heart to rest and community? If only these dreams could come true.

Here is a clarion call to our basics in caring for one another. In this day and age, we are not bound in any way to our small communities and limited horizons. We are citizens of a global order. We are independent in order to be interdependent. As the 'Phone Call' intimates, we are only a push button away from friends in the mountains of Tibet, to the jungles of Angola, or the plains of Siberia. Here, in verse, is a little of the hope for which we have been longing. In brief, in 'Chronicles of Light and Air' Australian theologian, educator, and activist, Denham Grierson, brings a fresh dimension to verse and its role in our human struggles. He gives expression to our feelings, anxieties, and dreams from basic, everyday life.

We live, in his words, into *'A bungee jump into a fearful nothingness'*. A jump that also opens up our lives to potential new beauties and inspirations. The most common experiences become magic as we let our minds and hearts collide over mere observations in, for example, observing a Wetland in nature. *"... All that we can hope for is laid out here. Stories of creation, narratives of species emergence, conquest, decline and fall, orchestrated dolefully by the deep chanting of the growling grass frog. Denizens of reeds and rushes that define boundaries of an ordered chaos, an undulating matrix that, peacock like, displays its beauty before me...'* The simplest moments become the most profound.

In other verses, we are challenged not to become techno prisoners of our time, allowing a mere phone call to rob us of more profound human experiences.

> *We are losing the gifts of gentle intimacy*
> *Stillness uncontaminated by insistent noise*
> *Multi-messages of communal reassurance beyond selfies*

> *The smell, the touch, the sounds of earth*
> *I pick up the wreckage (of a mobile phone thrown down)*
> *and put it in a skip*
> *Still shouting at us, accusingly, as we leave.*

Personally, I have known and loved Den. and Mavis for over fifty years. They have always been an inspiration in troubled times in Australia, the United States, and wherever the spirit of hope needs a word of encouragement. As a United Methodist Pastor in various congregations, I have found a warm reception from his words and insights. Folks just seem to 'connect' with Denham's ideas and expressions, and very fruitful conversations ensue! I continue to marvel at these moments of study and reflection.

In this volume, we are sometimes gently, and sometimes starkly, reminded that the weight of the world cannot be allowed to rob us of beauty, inside our own lives, and inside our natural settings. Life is sometimes a heavy lift, but our call to celebrate should never be bound up in pedestrian moments.

> *Life is overflowing*
> *No words suffice*
> *Resurrection Monday*
> *God's name be praised.*

Read and enjoy.

Thomas Gallen

Rev. Dr Thom. Gallen, author, social analyst, Church Executive, and Parish Minister, is an ordained member of the United Methodist Church in the United States of America.

Introduction

The poet John Burnside describes poetry as the music of time. W. H. Auden, for his part, believed poetry saved the world every day. Christopher Fry wrote, 'poetry is the language in which we explore our amazement'. Carl Sandburg, more mundane, says poetry is 'the opening and closing of a door'. For Shelley, poetry lifts the veil from the hidden beauty of the world, and he added, poets are the unacknowledged legislators of the world.

Shakespeare, unsurprisingly, states it convincingly.

> The form of things unknown, the poet's pen
> Turns them to shapes, and gives to airy nothing
> A local habitation and a name.
> (*A Midsummer Night's Dream* 5.1.15)

There is no end to such claims about poetry. To poets, Rainer Maria Rilke gave the advice, write because you must, understanding that you do not own what you write. We do what we must. And there is a mystery in this process. As Robert Frost admitted, 'I have never started a poem whose end I knew. Writing poetry is discovering'. (*New York Times*, 7 November 1957) Even recognising, as John Cage did, 'I have nothing to say and I am saying it and that is poetry' (*Silence* 1961).

However one seeks to understand poetry, the truth is that it comes unbidden into consciousness and insists on passing through to accomplish its work in the world. For a poet, it is neither good nor bad but necessary. Exploration of our humanness, trying to achieve existence clarification, addressing with varying success that which lies beyond comprehension but is the ground of all we see and know. This and much more.

The poems in this volume are explorations trying to unveil purpose and meaning in what has been called thick experience. There are many possible responses to what is written but each poem carries a gift to be received, and vistas to be discerned and contemplated. It is hoped they will do their work well. Whatever that is.

Acknowledgments

This book of poems found its way into the light by the efforts of a number of creative people. Hugh McGinlay edited the text with his usual precision and attention to detail. Nicci Douglas, with a midwife's care, followed it through the various stages of birth, and will continue its trajectory into the world of commerce.

My wife, Mavis, and my daughter, Su, made their usual contribution. My poet companions, John Cranmer and Andy Tiver, commented on, and argued adjustment to, many of the poems included, with their accustomed perception. Such a process required many extended lunches.

And my long-time friend and colleague, the Rev. Dr Thom Gallen, with the generosity which is characteristic of him, contributed a Foreword, with insight and social comprehension. My final thanks once again to Coventry Press.

The cocktail of gifts that has brought this book to completion has as its end a celebration of that festival we call life. We raise it together.

LIGHT

THOUGHTS OF LIGHT AND AIR

One thing that can change a person's life
Is a good story in the know
Offering new understandings of old certainties
Delivering unexpected possibilities
From small seeds forest towers grow

One can dive into deep stories naked
And emerge clothed in fresh fashions
Of thought, girded by nurturing risks
To take uncertain steps into unthought of actions

A bungee jump into a fearful nothingness
Only to return exuberant and changed
Wondering why it is not understood
The fall that births is upward

How slow the growing realisation
We are meant to shed dogma
As a snake sheds worn out skin
Clothed in new patterns of beauty
To become one of a cast of thousands

A LETTER TO MY GRANDSONS

The swaddling clothes of our humanity
Bind us more tightly than any Mummy
To a spacial realm, our moment in time
To humanness, to a sworn people
A family, a social group, a working crew
A community that shares one view - a given world

To become, in this pulsing complexity
Is not to conquer, be a success, a legend
But to enter into relation with the whole
With intentionality, to become oneself, for something
To be an integrity, a trust-worthiness, a presentness
That is uniquely you, a loved and loving somebody

And in the turmoil of existence
You will be approached, arrested, grasped
Addressed, seized, made attentive
By another who will ask of you
All that you will become and more
A commitment to say, I will one thing

This second binding is our escape from the first
A step into a wider freedom, to breathe a fresher air
Travelling into relationship across an unknown land
Without the means or skills to know this Other
Who turns yes and no into your brothers
And in each new adventure is the meeting

SONG

There are those religiously unmusical
Who do not feel the pulse of otherness
Transporting the coming day's offering
The chorus does not bring them solace

Vibrant colour enhancing all we see
Expectancy moving deep in our veins
Bliss celebrating this precious moment
With another, open to its immensity

Each breath a miracle, a glance-filled mystery
How can one dip one's hand in the stream
And not feel its meaning current-carried
Music of a hidden choir singing

Singing of blueness unending, carrying the soaring beat
Extolling a story of wonderment, old as granite tors
Exquisite as falling autumn leaves on virgin soil
Sprung from imaginative possibility

A garden where we go to look
Upon the tree of life branching inward
Waiting hearts hungry for the light's touch
The everlastingness of morning splendour

Here is the religious in the ground of things
Speckled bird flight, swift flash in the deep grass
Jazz in the afternoon sun
Perfume of jasmine on the summer air

Gentle embrace of numinous stillness
Pregnant with the coming secret of
The promises of tomorrow, spilling over
With sheer recklessness into freedom's gift

I cannot tell you of that pure sound
Vibrating throughout creation, shaping
Into a word astonishingly like a cosmic yes
In the swirling maelstrom of exploding atoms

All that black holes might devour
Cannot silence the song of the
world's giving, sung each day
As I begin my morning shave

SKINNED

The skin specialist was adamant
Apologetic without hope
The condition inescapably chronic
Nothing but to cope

My mind flooded with connections
All of them useless, obscene
Skin tight, skinflint
Thin skinned, skinned clean

No skin off, skins game
The verdict heavy on my shoulders
I returned from whence I came
Back to scratch

WARREN

The rabbit warren lay thirty metres
From the racing irrigation stream
Easy to divert a steady flow
Into the numerous holes of rabbit dreams

Harder to drive steel stakes the dray brought
Into the hard, dry, ravaged land
Stretching around them wire mesh, taut
Except for twenty yards where we would stand

The water ran without result all morning
At two-thirty in the desert strand
We stretched across the deadly opening
Axe handles held in eager hands

The first broke cover, then another
Hordes bursting forth into the waiting fence
The dogs without mercy turned barking to attack
Pandemonium of dust and swinging club defence

The battle joined at last, wide spread
Blood on our weapons, arms and legs
Dogs seizing rabbits, shaking heads
Hot summer sun poured on the dead

We laboured, covered with gore
Finally exhausted and done
One hundred, and twenty, and more
At our feet, unmoving, still as stone

There was no jubilation, only sadness
An enemy that ate vegetables, crop, and grass
Leaving the flock without resources
Bringing the farm to this decision at the last

Yet in the tough years of the war
We fed upon this vanquished foe
Rabbits had saved many of us from hunger
Now a harvest death had sowed

My brother afflicted by the task
Covered with dust and vivid welts
Rushed to a pinetarsal bath
We followed, hot, speechless, and spent

A pyrrhic victory we well knew
Other warrens close to hand
Rabbits have no word for few
Constantly breeding in erotic bands

The sheer necessity was clear
Farm life was to be saved
But after, in the farm house darkness
Their blood was running in my veins

SUPERMARKET

The cries for help get louder
    As the Supermarket doors
        Open to a rising cacophony
Shoppers with crumpled lists
    Confronting predatory shelves
        Bland, unmoving faces
Isolated, deaf to suffering
    Reaching the cavernous ceiling
        Bouncing back into inner caverns
A car brake screech barely heard
    In the consumer stamp of marching feet
        A young man puts biscuits up his shirt
His need crying out in an ice-field
    Of indifference, his entreaty lost in the wastes
        Tears of the city flow along saturated aisles

FADING

What is fading
        Is a sense of possession
                Of a known world
Taking our established security of identity
        With its chalk board eraser
                Leaving only faint trace
All of the certainties we gathered
        Misting away into a pale dawn
                Library books overdue
We fade with our images
        Shimmering in the mirror of the self
                Losing definition
What then can we hold as us
        Sliding away our generation vanishes
                Taking narratives that built cathedrals
It is not that we do not have stories
        No one is interested
                The diamond only a lump of coal quite deadly
We put on warm clothes and walking shoes
        Hold 55 year old married hands
                Mobiles carry our children's voices
We fade into this coming world
        Invisible, un-noticed, spirit source
                Of the hope and love they carry

A CONVERSATION WITH RILKE

Patience is all, you say
But each new day we are
At the starting line breaking
Before the starter's gun
Anxious for results, achievements, outcomes

The inner life grows slowly, you say
Carried to term according to its rhythm
As sap moves slowly in trunk and branch
So a poem comes on its own terms
Untroubled by time's insistence

I have thought of the creative process
As an aromatic, apple pie
Coming from the oven, needing only
To be placed on the page and
Cut in slices with delight

You must learn to let every feeling
And impression come to completion
The unsayable, the unconscious, the unattainable
Wait in deep humility for its coming
Learn every day, patience is all

JAZZ IN TIME

Polytonal harmony was the great idea
Leaping over racial and colonial deadness
Burrowing into inner reaches of spent-ness
Singing of a way of being free

A mixture of many colours, many moods
Exhibiting a time-space equilibrium
Not welcomed in classical symposiums
Hatching in nests of other broods

Harmony is always inclusivity
Balance moderates contra-puntal otherness
Gathering wild seeds from wind-swept wilderness
Planting in the centre unfolding unity

The one note, the one voice, the one truth
Sets fire to many fields of growing crops
Leaving in its wake shattered hearts at stop
No space for sparkle or nuance in its restricting touch

FIRST PEOPLE

They did not build cathedrals
Delineate sacred bounds
Define religion by structural status

All of the earth teemed with spirit-being
As did the cavalcade of stars above
Laid out as spiritual presence

In the Dreaming, land was alive
The people's life shaped inwardly
By resource of rock, water, gorge and plain

Stamping feet upon the deep red soil
Connecting with Mother-soul in corroboree
A given tribal identity from birth

No distinction between sacred and secular
Or physical or spiritual existence
Ceremonial, music, art and myth as one

With all created things one family
Embraced by the all-enfolding wonder
Of creation's bounty, givenness of grace

Living within eternity's wide womb
Made real in daily commerce, dance and song
Ochre painting of enchantment of this world's singularity

Rainbow snake dreaming, spirit birthing
At rest in the sea's song, the desert silence
Bound to each other as one people

TREASURE

The passing of years poses a task
To bring forth treasures old and new
Recognising a requirement of adaption
That will bring vitality to life anew

What to hold from what is old
How to choose from what is fresh
What to cast aside with courage bold
From the heritage of then, now mostly dross

The novel and the newly created
Flood into every corner with persistence
Drowning what past time has granted
Defining with optimism a new insistence

But neither new nor old survive
Without the nuance of the other's measure
Each enriches our daily lives
If only we knew which parts are treasure

CONFESSION IN A TIME OF SELF-ISOLATION

You would be granted
If you came with true remorse
Absolution from a priest
Sitting in isolation
On a parking lot chair
Making a ritual gesture
To your car in public space
Enabling you to return
To your isolation
Promised a broken relationship
Restored
Without visible assurance
Or evidentiary proof
In an environment of one

CRITICISM

There is a question to be asked
About criticism. Does it matter
Poetry is written to give expression
To an embryonic need. As personal
As a tooth brush. Not the possession
Of anyone but the poet, who knows that
He does not possess a word of any poem
Cast into the world. Each poem makes
Its way without him. He is only the medium
Of a travelling illumination

TOMORROW

We will be carried smoothly in electric cars
Responsive to our spoken commands
Feed by machines, houses cleaned by robots
Homes heated and cooled by programmed need
Appliances and lights controlled by vocal instruction
Entertained in virtual environments of many forms
Soothed by drug regimes, plastic adaption and enhancements
Dwellings fortified against unauthorised intrusion

Instructed, guided, reminded, assured, protected
Safe in our darkened cave staring at dancing shadows
Unmoved by risk, adventure, effort, achievement
Wondering at the slow dying of the light
Losing our life in the cocoon of pleasure's plenty
If we belong to the privileged and entitled it is so

Those not so blessed struggling for survival
Finding their life in scarcity and shared endeavour
Wind in their faces, rain on their fields
Facing daily hazard in nature's wide expanse
Companioned by joy, ambiguity, and forgiveness
In the testing of their humanness together
And the growth of their wings that lift them
Out of the cave into life

ISOLATION

You cannot be isolated
If someone is waiting
Active in your mind and heart
Conquering separation by treasured memory

Loneliness is a hunger not met
By solitary mirror images
A deep emptiness
Unfilled by the caring touch of another

If we are hollow
We will not have peace
Miss the tide rising into
A quiet pool of reflection

Where the music of times past
Fills the air with magic
Soothing distress
Carrying the heart safely to rest

COMING

We are falling down
Into a plastic drowned lake
Filled with bric-a-brac
From which our leaders drink
Ingesting nano particles
Making them more plastic
Every day, gifted by affluence
With the appearance of newness
As deadly as the shine
Upon the red-bellied black
Moving slowly towards me

MORNING

Old bloke in his dressing gown
Moving in his much loved cave
Another day of ups and downs
Breakfast first and then a shave

Munching, watching petals fall
From a late autumnal rose
Looking for a cumquat ball
A tissue for a runny nose

Watching growing Winter clouds
In a bright and shiny sky
Reading a Psalm out loud
Answering how, what and why

TIMING IS EVERYTHING

The glass of wine
Was disquieting
Poured too early
Heavy wind and rain
Outside
The day unsettled

Of a dark inky demeanour
Deep blood red
In afternoon light
Blood associated
Blood informed
Blood redeemed

Poured too early
Before time of repentance
Un-breathed
Deeds not fulfilled
Taste uncompleted
Prayer not offered

Poured prematurely
Wine unspilled
Lacking embodiment
Before life was lived
Needing redemption
Timing is everything

There is a given timeliness
Season of harvest
Full grape to crusher
Long darkness dwelling
Tasting in vintage light
Timing is everything

Poured in fulfilment
Time conquered
Time captured
Time poised
Then the forgiveness
The waiting completeness

GUARDIANS

The public guardians are not trustworthy
Consumed by desire for power
We lack not safety, but vision
That lifts the darkness of the present hour

The guardians we trust are not eminent
They come vacuum and bucket in hand
To clean and dust, working with enjoyment
Cheerful, humble, without pretensions to be grand

In them a working class directness
Constancy and caring in all they touch
Checking that our actions are not reckless
Sharing their vision of life is to share and not to poach

UNIVERSITY OF THE THIRD AGE

Put me down, add my name
List me as a joiner
If required, in the game
Whether as a senior or a junior
My excuses seem so lame
I wished I had acted sooner
That always was my aim
The goal of a consumer
Commitment of both heart and brain
One question of good humour
Is this the group for sinks and drains
Or those for playing tubas

JUGGLER

We are all jugglers now
Trying to keep in balanced alignment
Images from our chaotic social space
Disparately connected in empty merriment

Held in consort by constant momentum
Energy shaped by gravity's tyrannous pull
Continual demand on us to be productive
A willed intensity of purpose drill

This is an epiphanic field collection
A juggling in the context of our time
Leaving space alluringly for options
Unavailable in the constant pantomime

So frantic the requirement to succeed
To keep in active play a sense of duty
Rising, flying, returning, insisting
Exhausting in their importunity

It is a feat beyond mere entertainment
To hold a purposed enterprise aloft
Against a featureless, undefined nothingness
Is it time to stop? Go home for tea or not

MOTHER

Dark circled eyes, red cheeks, high temperature
Anxiety rises in a time of virus
Ringing the doctor, sudden departure
So swiftly the moment of crisis

Tests are taken, results reassure
Fear and worry drain away
She tells the doctor, he is only four
More grateful than she can say

Driving slowly home, swept by tiredness
Conscious of some shame, some doubt
Ignoring the strain, lifting him regardless
Praying he does not have another bout

Tucking her son in bed, single, alone
Some water in his glass, a Panadol
Sitting with a coffee after, an inner moan
Rises unbidden from her mothering soul

LETTING GO

At the University of the Third Age gathering
Jessup waxed lyrical
All that matters, truly matters, he said
You can pack into a knapsack

Your life, that part which carries its essence
You can lift easily
As you step out each day
Beginning again

The first half of life is gathering together
The second half is letting most of it go
To hold fast to essential things matters
It is a relief to see all else slip away

Looking at the chalk in his hand
He turned to the blackboard
We need space to breath in
The life we have lived

Taking the eraser he wiped the black board
Clean
This, said Jessup, is the time for reading
Between the lines

THE COLOUR OF THE WIND

Poetry is the impish attempt to paint the colour of the wind.
Maxwell Bodenheim

Not entirely one would say, add
To shape and mould the day

To craft patterns on the water
And give mirth to easy laughter

To bring falling rain to eagle down
And reverence to a puckish frown

To sketch upon the evening breeze
Give inspiration to a cunning wheeze

Or to add to gravitas
A touch of human habitat

Leaping o'er a drifting moon
To beat hurry to too soon

The magic of the inner eye
That tells what lives, what moves, what dies

CLIVE JAMES

He wrote like no one else, did Clive James
Unique in style, an inspired amalgam of classical
Ironical, bogan earthiness, wit and whimsical artistry
So captivating that each new book a feast to delight in
A juggler casting dancing metaphors into the sunlit air
A magician's sleight of hand holding you in suspense
Bringing you beyond illusion to a new awareness
He told stories and made commentary of wondrous design
An addiction to listen to his knowing, chuckling voice
His last book of poems shed a twilight gloom
On an old, sick man, stumbling with disease
Filled with remorse and bone deep guilt
For what he called deceit and faithlessness
Trying to find forgiveness for moral failure
To those he loved, to those he had betrayed
Lacking resources to assuage his pain
Coming to his end without hope of redemption
Hearing now no applause but the silence of judgment
His poems, as magical as ever, he falling defeated into darkness

BELLS

I heard bells in the sharp morning air
Today
Other-worldly, a language out of time
Ethereal
Bringing to a halt all other sounds
Chimeingly

For what can compete with the summons of
Eternity
Crystal purity in carriage and tonal
Weightlessness
Assuring us of the rhythm of our lives, resonating
Within
I listened to the bells calling today
Wondering
Asking the question, What are they telling
Tolling

STATUS

We stepped cautiously down the slope
Between raised furrows
Flowing towards the nearby stream
Sharp smell of fertiliser and dug earth following

Elias was bent over, hands deep in the soil
Hearing our approach the old man turned
A delighted smile swept his weathered features
Shakily, he rose and spread his arms wide

I would give you a hug
But my hands are dirty
Be at ease, Elias, Jessup said
None of us has clean hands

MORNING WALK

Masked, winter coated figures move anonymously
Along the edges of the wetlands
Scuttling before the brisk wind like
Fallen leaves discarded by re-stocking trees

Overhead dark scowling clouds threaten
Insulted by the impudence of this herded group
Being out in the open without stamped permits

The clouds are ignored, it being agreed the wind
Will send them to another quarter
Where they can scowl and sulk at will

Weather occupies the walker's conversation
That perennial topic that fills blank spaces
Without offence or meaning, and if weather
Fails to entertain, there is always the football
With fleeting concern about mounting injuries

It is as if this ritualised agenda casts a heavy cloak
On the pond's surface where every effort is
Being made to smooth out the wind's scarring
And to give protection to the swan's nest
where, viability in the balance, the signets
Are late in season

A struggle always part of this scene's contours
The rawness of earth and sky and water
Exacting a toll for permission to view its splendour

Change that comes slowly we can embrace
Suddenness is not to be contemplated
The tree branch falls unexpectedly upon him
A trip down the steps, a slip of feet on black ice

All unimagined disasters in a blink of an eye
As a pandemic, whose seriousness was not admitted
Until death stalked homes, institutions and
Aged care. Protesters claim it is not so

What then to talk of with the hooded host
Escaping isolation and boredom. Existence, threat
And death score no interest alongside morning melodies
Bingo and cards

You cannot expect applause when confronting the real
Which for all the beauty of another wind-swept morning
Is profoundly present in this unquiet landscape
Filling hollowness with its persistent beat
Asking us for dialogue, a meeting

PARABLE

There are seed pods in every thriving plant
Deep in the water of the slowing stream
Hundreds of seeds, packed in rows
Waiting for summer warmth, orders to invade

To seed, to grow, to multiply, choking the open channels
With bunched up, impassioned spreading plants
Leaving no place for passage, no clear way
Suffocating with abundance, conquering where they may

Sparkling water, as if frozen ice, moving at glacial pace
Diverted into hard, vanishing spaces, shackled to excess
Momentum arrested, disappearance of means and ends
A slow winding down into darkened morass

With spade and rake, we strain to clear the blockages
Opening up small outlets, digging plants away
Removing obstructions, all suppressing water's laughter
Seeing again increasing flow, recovery of freedom's play

PERSPECTIVE

You are not wanted here, he said
Old slippers and World War anecdotes
Belong in the cupboard and the bottom drawer
We are not domicile in your ancient dwelling

We are conceiving new worlds
Imagining and re-imagining the human
In a global matrix of becoming
That has no interest in arcane sermons

We are quick-silver selves
Sparking off primal sources
Going where no one has gone before
Co-creating star-bound entities

Keep out of the way
The time of homespun philosophies is past
You are mechanical litter in an electronic age
With desiccated wisdom no longer saleable

There is nothing more that you can offer
Do us the respect of getting out from underfoot
And take your memories and your back pack with you
Leaving I heard the kookaburra laugh

WHERE OR WHEN

The flugal horn played the jazz classic softly
Where or when
Its enchantment inviting us into mystery
Across zones of imagined experience

Instrument expressing the musician's gift
Honed to its perfection
By endless hours of persistent graft
Emerging slowly, painfully, and beautifully

Is it true, it asks, we have before
Been in this moment
Relived again in recollection
By musical magic, a sense of wonder

Behind the trumpeter a dedicated quartet
Veterans of such sets
Bound together by their love of music
Their achievement fruit of a cost gladly met

Transporting us into a rapture of delight
Repeating remembered sounds
Uncertain, as the vocals say
Of where or when

CHILD

It came to me suddenly
That time is a child newborn
How else could it be
When now is a beginning

We are the teachers
Our lives the content
That fills the hoar frost vacuum
Of time's emptiness

We are the ones whose stories
Satisfy the waiting hunger
To be known and named
Lest the past come before something forms

Time does not pass us by
But carries us in its forming
Of new things, new futures, new nows
When we again tell timeless tales

VOICE

It is your voice we will miss
First lost in the palliative shroud
When drugs were withdrawn
And now forever silent

We will miss its gentle reassurance
Its touch of healing and care
That arose from a heart open
Sensitive, embodying hospitality

We will miss the memories it evoked
Of shared ventures, the tones of hurt
And struggle, courage and forgiveness
And its trustworthy steadfastness

We will miss your voice
For it carried to us your integral self
A fullness of encompassing love
That in dark times we trusted implicitly

We must learn to live with silence now
But we are not totally bereft
The cadence of your life remains
We will hear your voice always

HERE AND THERE

He died suddenly, the cancer virulent
With little warning, a lightning flash
As deadly as those igniting forest fires
Strong, healthy, athletic, a life full of intent

Lost in that vortex we call death
Whose presence we strive to ignore daily
Traffic accidents, mud slides, cyclones
Abstract newspaper reports, not breath

Expiring, hope evaporating, life disappearing
In the blink of an eye, stone dead
Laid among death-denying monuments
Blind, deaf, as memorial bells ring

Born into a world abruptly
An existence rich beyond telling
Why fear another step beyond
Into a waiting, receiving us gently

MAGICIAN

He cast his spell with clear intention
Magically with words creating worlds
Into which we travelled willingly
Enchanted by the mystery half-believed

A swirl of the red-lined cape called
Into being and equally caused to vanish
Trajectories that enticed into futures
Promising riches beyond illusion

I was a believer, not in the effects
But in the mystery that lay behind this
Pale shadow of reality, deep in the fibres
Of my being, convinced somewhere a treasure lay

The magic lay in the enthusiastic delight
Of the conjurer in his art
Pointing as it did in its fantasy and conceit
To the true ground behind the gesture and the call

PHONE CALL

The smashed mobile phone
Lay broken in the gutter
Here lies, said Jessup
Mid-wife, au pair, butler, guardian
Mentor, therapist, companion on the way
Prison of our victimhood

Without it we feel lost, abandoned, forsaken
Lacking a breast to provide nourishment
Pleasure, excitement, stimulation gone
Persuasive design no longer in our grasp
The cost we pay too high to name
A vanishing of our power to see

We have lost access to natural beauty
The splendour of nature's music blocked out
Time woven into the literature of the ages
The quest within our doubt, smothering
Warm community with old friends
Shared memories, bonds that define our ends

We are losing the gifts of gentle intimacy
Stillness, uncontaminated by insistent noise
Multi messages of communal reassurance beyond selfies
The smell, the feel, the touch, the sounds of earth
I picked up the wreckage and put it in a skip
Still shouting at us, accusingly, as we leave

ANOTHER TIME, ANOTHER PLACE

Lunch at an old friend's place
Was to enter another world
Of cobbled lanes and narrow streets
That, like spider trace, lived off
The broad limbs of public roads

Twisting and turning among workers' cottages
Along bypaths obscure and secret
Where muttered instructions, covert orders
Were given to messengers with hooded lanterns
Following agendas of the night

I listened for the clop of muffled hooves
Looked for horse droppings at ancient corners
A proud belonging in complex networks
Of a neighbourhood of sealed lips
And ironclad loyalties, tribal loyalties

Suddenly one is cast into a square
Council uplifted with architectural polishing
A shiny plaque declaring beside a water fountain
'Dedicated in 1867 for community use'
Under the gaze of two-storeyed gentrified dwellings

Bluestone fences topped by iron grills
Leading along tessellated paths to high gloss doors
Testifying to garages filled with Volvos and Land Rovers
Passing by the hidden life of worker cottages
Unaware, certainly not comprehending, an invisible host

Here quiet people live who drink at the community fountain
Renovating their timber dwellings with care

Chiselling old values into restoration with fierce zealotry
Keeping picket fences white and memory of another time
Young couples, refugees from upwardly mobile squares

Moving away from old gas lights on tall iron poles
I plunge back into the labyrinth of streets and lanes
Arriving at last, hearing the distant noise of modern traffic
That has little efficacy here where I sit stamped, 'Visitor
Duration Three Hours'. Stranger in a strange land

LISTEN

Listen to the suffering wind
Howling beast of Spring design
Baying to a gibbous moon
Enemy of all that's mine

Seeking to escape the torment
Of a desecrated earth
Monstrous wave of anguish
At a despising of its worth

Auger as a murder of crows
Weakening each tree's resolve
Wanting answers for our crime
Virus of a warming globe

Moaning with a hidden pain
Shouting for a healing balm
We must understand again
We were meant to do no harm

TIDE

The rip corkscrews away
Arrowing to deeper water
Capturing the unwary
The not attending

Go with its urgency
Seek its edge
Be carried into deep water
Escape into fathomless possibility

Learn to swim in ambiguity
Buoyed by the tide
That you cannot control
But carries you to your destiny

The illusion of freedom
Will remain intact
Unseen currents
Will do their work

Out into the open place
Seized by the unknown
There before your awareness
Waiting for your coming

ABANDONMENT

To give something up. Not to own it. To set it free
A bird liberated from a trap
A thought loosed from dogma
Ariel of trust. Not to hold. Not to possess

Owning only a sense of self. Nurturing vocation
Putting aside all else
Life thinned and fallow
Freedom not to hold, not to own, not to possess

Beginning anew each day. The distant cry
Calling us to ceaseless praising
Within the confines of a birthing earth
Telling, do not hold. Do not own. Do not possess

LET IT GO

You cannot lift what is too heavy
Avoid collapse of what was strong and true
There is no point in futile rage
Put it down. Let it go

It is a mirage to believe that you will win
Fighting by an act of will, heroically
That which it is impossible to change
Be at rest. Let it go

Chose to accept, and accepting rise
Above conditions as implacable as death
Float above a fated necessity
By choosing to be free. Let it go

MEASURE

They never got the measure of Jesus
Nor have we, clothing him in cultural cliches
Turning him into a cipher, salesman of pedagogic saws
Multiplying images in countless guises

He escapes all our needy declarations
Since he does not live in the conferred
Flowing like water into our fictions
Enigmatic in every gesture, every word

Eternally elusive to our gaze and thought
For none of our measuring devices suffice
None can tally wisdom, compute whimsey
Who can predict roll of the dice

If I had met him then he would be silent
Quietly amused at my bewilderment
Here would be an unasked question
An unspoken answer to predicament

When I greet him now he says, grow up
Get on with your task, as I did mine
It is time you came of age, become adult
We will join along the way in act and sign

So we must learn not to lean upon
A time-trapped phantom, long since moved on
Into the entanglement of creation
Deep within our beating heart, under our sun

RAIN

I await the coming rain
Lightning flash and thunder roll
Promise of the life we live
Turning dust bowls into pools

Then shall the earth delight
In the rebirth of the plains
Dry creek beds gather water
Guardians of what sustains

The sound grows nearer, louder
Accompanied by festive drums
Overhead the battered roof
Thrums and thrums and thrums

And I am once again renewed
Listening to the heavens fall
Life of my life in each drop
Symphony that sings and calls

CREPE-MYRTLE

Crepe-myrtle brown leaf clad
Slowly giving up pretence of beauty
Grieving past summer glory

KNOWLEDGE

It is a conceit we carry
That if we acquire knowledge
We will reign supreme

Over a century the Gifford lectures
Gathered the brightest minds together
A magnificent company that resolved little

The blue wren on the wire
Beyond the window sill
Is more sovereign than us

He knows the virtue of simplicity
The measure of flight, how to
Trust in the order of things

GRASSHOPPERS

On the track from farmhouse to road
A morning task to collect the newspaper
Grasshoppers mustered in marshalled ranks
Scouts sent out in large numbers
Attacking my bare legs with insistence

Across paddocks they flew in squadrons
Wings glinting menacingly in morning sun
Happy to absorb abundant losses
Coming on, coming on, coming on
Stripping the earth of its vitality

My shirt and shorts covered with crawling bodies
Sandals squashing multiple patrols
Occupying sandy stretches of the path
Filling the air with grasshopper OMs
I could not find the paper in the flak

Walking back along the track, harassed
I watched their army cross the land
Demolishing precious plants and crops in turn
Across the serried vales, hunger rampant
Consuming by necessity our life

HARD RUBBISH PICK-UP

Hard rubbish collections grow on nature strips
Tired, broken, rejected items droop in groups
Wheelbarrow, kitchen chairs, fans, buckled blinds
A queen sized mattress full stop to saddened routes

A sense of recognition, status shared
Discarded objects thrust rudely aside
Echoes in unsteady feet and watery eyes
Passing these graveyards with slowing stride

Stamp upon the whole reads, obsolete
Time travelling on, with unsentimental sweep
Tomorrow, trucks will come, debris carried away
Relief will sweep the streets, escaping reality's display

WETLANDS

The wetlands were waiting
Ducks in a row
Swallows dipping across
Unwrinkled water
White Egret, statue still
Moorhens scratching a living

Despite heavy pedestrian traffic
On the water
There was placidness
Friends playing cards
Licking ice-creams
Watching sunset in silence

The sadness is
We must pass by
Although feeling acceptance
In the warm evening gloom
Participation means waiting, trusting
We are not good at that

SHADOW

I looked for the shadow
Of his passing
Too late to see, to hold
Where then the shadow's footprints

MOMENTS

A leaf upon a trickling stream
Reflections in the mirror's gleam
Baby on a playground swing
Chalk symbols on a blackboard sing

Damper in a fireside glow
Letters in a scrabble show
Rolling waves upon the shore
Pelicans drifting as before

Waving from a passing train
Initials in wet concrete lain
Apples not far from the tree
Magpies making corroboree

Shadows in the morning sun
Chorus of a song begun
Road leading to a distant run
Breathing deeply, having fun

Sunscreen on sun-burnt skin
Shivering from an early swim
Owl brush in a darkening scene
Telling stories of a time that's been

Strands bound together, memory spun
Small moments from remembering won
Guitar vibration along tightened strings
The endless joy that sharing brings

WAKING IN FRIGHT

Slipping away, elusive as a forgotten name
It is the terror of drowning in wheat
Oates lost forever in Antarctic sleet
Fear of failing to deliver
Blank pages when all is over
Trying to banish shame

Are we always to be bewildered
By instructions to be managed
Dependent on itineraries, and lights to change
Coldness causing us to shiver
Temperature rising to a fever
Uncertain of conclusions oft derided

Always in the gloom, approaching light
Amongst green leaves in the orchard
Swelling fruit, both soft and hard
Rain drifting into every crevasse
Leading us out of our impasse
Reassuring as to a child, waking in fright

ONCE UPON A TIME

Once upon a time
When monsters threatened
Heroes rose to overcome them

Once upon a time
Rulers respected law
And served all the people

Once upon a time
Respect and civility thrived
And streets were safe

Once upon a time
One's word was one's bond
Employers paid just wages

One upon a time
People acted as one
And loved one another

Honour and justice prevailed
Hope and peace true options
Once upon a time

TODAY

We are like a besieged city
Surrounded by dark forces
Awaiting orders to advance

Life goes on in small dwellings
Food is shared, stories told
Under a sulking sky of menace

It is difficult to escape a sense of doom
Even the returning swallows are
Not building nests in the eaves this year

Our feet negotiate broken stones
We breathe air clouded with deceit
Everything important falsified in language

We are suffocating with things
Dire prophesies circulate unchallenged
Circuses do not perform

It is a time for gathering
To share eternal verities
To remember promises forgotten

WEST WIND

The west wind, recognising no equals
Howled across basalt plains
The rocky foundation fragmenting under
Assault from sun and wind

This was not a time for speech
Frozen tongues soundless, stopped mouths
Silent until the fall of twilight when
The wind rested a while after its merciless scouring

How blessed we are, we said to each other
Air, crisp, clean, cold around us
Calling us to adventure, unexplored territory
Pointing to hidden realms to be explored

That was the way of it when we were young
Carried by the insistence of spirit
Driven by questing intentionality
To seek resolution and home's beckoning safety

Now we rest, the wind scolding
And squabbling around stone corners outside
While we contemplate long journeys over
Saying to each other, how blessed we were

IMPRESSION

Perceiving what it is
Is no small task
More than human
Less than divine
Lively daemonic presence
With kindly intent of will
Lost in a swirl of randomness
Bound tight by centred purpose
Surrounding us, impenetrable
In opening up engagement
Requiring rationality
In Dionysian draughts
At once impossibly
Nurturing the possible
Time entering space
Space stretching time
All at once
And not at all
Suspended between
Now and then
Fugitive of thought
Escapee from insight's grasp

APPLE TREE

White petal rain across wetland pools
Signalling the end of autumn's reign
Vacuumed from the clusters of tree branches
By winter's determined administration

Stripping to sweep bare all that was
Harsh jagged claws of predatory winds
Employed to clear out all trace
Of what was good and true and beautiful

Without success. Opulent yellow wattles
Leading a rebellion against the cold breath of righteousness
Poverty itself is not the curse, but abandonment
Of multiple forms of life, defenceless, small, unique

On the unpromising slope an ancient apple tree
Holds firm before the blast, dropping apples
That fall not far, seed bearers
Waiting in trust for the coming impulse of Spring

SCARRING

All of us have scarring
From wounds we never sought
Where unexpected kindnesses
Healed grief we thereby caught

Never in the plan of things
Nor entertained in thought
Innocence despoiled
Suffering without support

Blows destined to sort us out
No explanation of anguish brought
In time we learn to see its gain
Strength we never could have bought

Unveiling in a backward way
The pathway being taught
Gifting a nascent pilgrimage
By means hidden and covert

LOOKING GLANCE

I look for the translucent glow
Beneath the chosen words on show
Something precious, something eternal
Knowing the colour will not be purple
Royal the hammer and the axe
Discarded treaties, broken pacts
Looking for the hidden glow
In all the certainties I know
Wondering at the stylised speech
Unsure what they seek to reach
Always a stranger in the crowd
Unknowing in the holy cloud
Why do they love the lowest rung
When they have heard Messiah sung
Strange that at the earliest dawn
We hear the distant, calling horn
Knowing that at the break of day
Our footsteps walk a chosen way
Turning in time, both quick and slow
I look for the translucent glow

INTERMISSION

WETLAND

The wetland ponds have decided
No one knows how or when
That Winter and Summer will be honoured
By calm, harmonious surfaces
That mirror-like reflect the sky
Passing clouds pausing to check hair
And dress as they pass on their way

The first, casting chill silence across
Still water gone dark and pensive at its touch
Immobile with a deep petulance that
Is to be found in arrested movement
Cold calculation, and suppression of all
Manifestations of undisciplined life

The second, celebrative, a travelling minstrel show
All colour, light and laughter in bright sun
Flocks of birds cohabiting across glassy water
Gentle drift across rippling surfaces
A fullness of time and place, satiated
Content at the completion of its watch
Clapping hands at darting swallows closing off the season

Autumn and Spring are a different matter
Not at ease with order-shape across the ponds
Already stirring adolescent disorder over
A quiescent landscape, seething and teeming underneath
Novelty and inventiveness bubbling into wakefulness
Determined to change the set order of the world
Contriving stupendous stunts and japes for the tomorrow

The first turning the environment into a palette of colour
Shaking loose from trees elaborate garments of leaves
That have contrived to hide the Emperor's nakedness
Agitating the ponds with noisy, buzz-saw winds
Throwing into the air a miasma of tints and shades
Blocking culverts and drains, writing graffiti
On the clouds with dark smoke from burning piles

The second is never still, bursting forth as dramatically
As the Demon King, midwife to the new generation
Sending vitality along branches, shoots, into the heart
Of all living things, compelled to wake up from hibernation
To greet a new day, sending across hill, valley
And lake, wind storms and rain, imperious and demanding
Calling into being a uniqueness that has been before

Gazing across the wetlands it is inescapable
That time's layers have sharp differentiation in
The changing light and tumbling variation
The now, of course, this moment of bird-chick softness
Within the nest of the day, early with promise and energy
Now being called home to bed by a twilight sky
Within the numbered repetition of a week's nurturing

Stretching out to months and years and
Decades, and centuries into an endless
Mystery of once upon a time when all things
Began to move to a hidden impulse
That included potentially the fecund wetlands that
Learned sobriety enough to craft this moment
Where I seek to read its ancient text

A text of multiple languages, of countless tribes
Of rising and falling, loss, suffering, death
Rebirth, cascading variety, a pattern
Of conformity in the wilding chaos of new birth
Another day following, bringing possibility and demand
Across a stretch of water where beauty
And terror are old caretaker acquaintances

All that we could hope for is laid out here
Stories of creation, narratives of species emergence
Conquest, decline and fall, orchestrated dolefully
By the deep chanting of the growling grass frog
Denizen of reeds and rushes that define
Boundaries of an ordered chaos, an undulating matrix
That, peacock-like, displays its beauty before me

You can debate, if you will, here is the child of chance
Or the emergence of an evolving universe, a purposed
Process shaped by spontaneity and creative will
The pattern of an eternal Tao, the touch of
A creative God, explanations that do not
Enhance or diminish what is here displayed
A cornucopia of wondrous devising

It is what it is, a tantalising, fey creation
Carrying within its gift multiple worlds in
Which we may play with delight
Spelling out all of the possibilities this small
Planet offers to those who come at twilight
To hear the music, watch setting light give
Dying colour to its canvas

Tomorrow, if I come again, it will be different
But arguably the same in its hospitality
I will watch and wait and ask of it
How is it that we are so fortunate to have
Within our untrustworthy grasp this stupendous, boundless
Explosion of fullness, enfolding us, as if by right
Into the embracing love of God's eternity

TAP DANCE

Suddenly
Without prior intent
She began to tap dance
Because she wanted to
Dance breaking free
From its subliminal hiding place
Every atom of her body alive
Hair flying
Head twisting
Arms waving
Fingers clicking
Legs shaking
Feet tapping urgently
Laughter spilling over
A cadenza of delight
An extravagant ecstacy
All of her together
In outrageous joyousness
That is the way it is
Sometimes

WETLAND REPRISE

The wetlands are our gift
Wrapping around our village
Glistening ponds interlaced
Spread with bird chorus
In convocation at twilight
With messages of different kinds
Different import, different languages
Mysteriously arising from soft throats
In sharp-uttered choirs haphazardly arranged
A world in which terror and death
Stalk defenceless offspring mercilessly

Reminding us of mortality and the
Inexorability of life's hazard
Over still water, intimations of mist rising
Water weeds not able to muffle communications
Ephemeral. Swallows, expert sky dancers
Dart across wide expanses of surface
Whispering of open air where thought gestates
Freely without prohibition and agendas
The outcome of cramped minds and
Avaricious hearts without gentleness and love

There is no ending to this songfest
Rich tellings from a fertile world
Renewing itself with harmony
That is not manufactured but rises
Unselfconsciously from inner roots
Soul-sustenance from deep in earth's

Fire that does not sign branded ownership
On the cool, collected surfaces of the pond's
Beauty, stretching its arms across plants
And trees, benediction upon the flowing
Life on the water, speckled with
Swarms of insects parted by a
Marauding owl in the gathering dusk

The day writing up events so that
Tomorrow will not forget what has to be spoken
Has to be sung, has to be celebrated, has
To be shared. Listening for the social chatter of
Night birds in the darkness gossiping
There is a reassuring heartbeat heard
Which runs through all life, celebrating in this
Hallowed space, creation's love of all
Its children in a wideness filled with delight
The fragrance of the earth, and God's outgoingness

LESSON

It is a lesson learned early
Some questions have no answers
Perhaps they do
But we will not know them

We are confronted by this inevitability
That we will not know
That what we know, itself
Is part of this unknowing

We exist in a stream of unknowing
Getting by, trial and error stumbling
With the help of friends
In a world of seeming randomness

Asking, seeking, knocking
Trying to make sense
Of a world we do not understand
And never will, completely

Draw up a list. Of uncertainty
volatility, variability, incompleteness
Chance, chaos, disorder
Opaqueness, ineffability, unexpectedness

Here on the raft amid flowing insecurity
What can we know
That will stand inviolate
Not vitiated by time's obscurity

AIR

The answer is learned early
Our first, true ground is trust
That acceptance of thisness
Surrounded by a sea of care

Whatever time's incomprehensibility
Bewildering in all its forms
Acceptance in trust is all we have
And all we need

SHINING

In a gigantic block of marble
Michelangelo found David hiding
Un-flung pebbles not yet formed
Destiny not yet presiding

They were shot down in the street
Women, children with no rating
Regarded as disposable
Not worthy lives for sculpturing

Never to emerge from hiding
Potential in them, fading
Teapots filled with loving succour
Poured out upon dry earth, dying

This is what is hard to bear
The lost, the not called forth, the passing
Consider the beauty, the majesty of David
Oh, so much never brought to shining

THE SEASON OF PLAGUE

The season of plague
    Is a time of unburdening
        For that is the gift of loneliness
Locked down space shuts off air
    Through masks preventing aspiration
        Clearing memory's sand for revisiting
Not much else is available
    Or necessary in the quiet nights
        Relieved of detritus
Only the centre intensifies
    Only the heart beat sounds
        Only the stillness heals
Time for planting fresh seeds
    Old and new tears mingled
        Borning a startled self-awareness
An overthrowing of a world view
    Can grow a searching heart
        Unexpectedly fertile
Weighing the light and air
    Counting the stars appearances
        Opening night on a play of purposes
Because of a plague of reckoning
    Providing solitary time
        To fashion a bouquet from pain and threat
Drawing perfume from
    A crop of fresh flowers
        Whose promise is now kept

A LIFE IMAGINED

There is more myth than history
In the Gospel's staged inventiveness
More imaginative projection than mere fact
In the narrative of this life journey
A setting of a way, minimalist in form
Enlarged by reflection, a maximalist intent
In order to give substance to his otherness

Myth is not right or wrong
It is either living or dead
Not black script on a page
But riotous colour of vitality
A rolling film of action
That gives inner meaning
Missed if rigid within a literal frame

Here is the inwardness of what we know
Not a pale sketch of happening events
Nor a chronicle list proscribed
Rather the warm flow of human contact
Spirit skipping in and out of possibility
Carried in a flesh and blood contest of life
Inviting us beyond reverence to celebration

DECONSTRUCTION

It is the curse in us
That having planted magic beans
We climb the huge trunk to its height
And besiege the castle of the giant

Not caring for proprieties of the border
We invade his castle, home, and order
Steal his goose and harp
And scuttle down the mottled bark

Then crime on crime, we chop down
The beautiful, majestic tree
Precipitating the giant's death
Adding murder to our crimes beneath

A fable of deceit and pillage
As if the stranger, the freak, the other
Has no claim to our respect
It is our right to steal and wreck

Despoiling what is not ours
Conquering both strong and weak
In the name of empire and honour
Sowing hate, reaping horror

A fairy tale embodying
Patterns and ways at school
Laying out the planning
For those born monstrously cruel

Regard Jack of the beanstalk
Creature of the dark
Celebrated for his cleverness
A life of savage ruthlessness

FROM FAR AWAY

What is it that we bring with us from far away
Gathered in our knapsack for emergencies
To be explored, understood, expanded, used
Although we are not sure ownership belongs to us

A matter of investigation and hard falling
Traversing uncertain ground with dubious support
Trying to discern what it is we carry
Within the turmoil of slow building of thought

As from the magician's hat, surprising things
Unanticipated and unknown, discovered in
Need and pain and wandering in dark woods
Unsure of the way that leads to otherness

To stretch out a hand is wondrous
Slow unfolding of the given aids
We find within our gift, in timeliness
Ready for the snow flake's fall, the rising sun

UNNAMEABLE

We were given words to name the world
Land, sea, air, creatures of these realms therein
Residents of endless skies, time spun and space spin

We use words to define outside
Fossick within consciousness as well
Dimensions that we hold and tell

We name ourselves, and others like ourselves
By gift of speech, a self to each
Stamping identity in baptismal reach

But words have no power to name
Beyond event horizons unknown otherness
A terminus is reached, a trackless wilderness

More than elusive, more than beyond our grasp
A void bewildering to cognition
A nothingness defying all prescription

Light beyond sun, life beyond rain
Generic beyond flesh, spirit beyond flight
Essence of imagination's maps, darkness beyond night

We fall endlessly into this lighted abyss
Rise into space beyond all reckoning
Immerse ourselves in uncanny pondering

Words are no more than signs
Pointing to what we cannot tell
Re-defining an unfathomable well

Air, wind, a breathless brush
Stillness without form or presentness
Silence of creation's nothingness

Out, afar, beyond, forever
Within, bottomless, closeness begun
Unnameable, escaping words, the One

TREE

Crossing the worn threshold once more
Of the night's violence and uncaring
Stretched out upon the path, dying
The old, loved tree lay slain by a Spring storm

All of its delight, dancing green leaves
Filled with hope of tomorrow's day, gone
Limbs no longer capable of playful games
Catastrophe of seeping blood and broken bones

Who granted life to me in gentle greeting
As I came home each day depleted
By blankness, a deep down retreating
No longer a presence, except of the departed

Tree, you were a mother's love to me
Whispering of God's eternity in late light fall
Flinging a eucalyptus charm upon the air
Sorrow rising like a mist, a darkening pall

SACRED SPACE

We are not seduced by time
No heavy weight of history
Bows our shoulders down
No imperial remembrance of things past
Reverence of Kings and National fame

It is space that beguiles us
In a timeless land
First people lightly care-taking
Vast distances of ochre dust

Unfolding identity from rocks and trees
Embracing Mother Earth, unfailing care
Writing on the wind of sacred place
Only the ancient eye, the dancer sees

Dreaming a world of spirit being
Filled with the presence of otherness
Life-filled mountains, oceans, deserts, streams
A living in, a living with, a special seeing

A land of brutal contrast, shifting moods
Criss-crossed map of tribal knowing
We lift our eyes to what is given now
In famine, fire, tempest and floods

Spread mantle of wholeness over all things
Entering into the membrane that silence brings
A distant vista, a sudden glimpse
Our hearts rise up on enchanted wings

There is deep in the earth a throbbing beat
Music of a time, eons before time began
We feel it in the fibre of our being
It fills us with its gift through dancing feet

There is no permitting stamp of time, no leather tomes
Chronicles of this land's history of blood and gore
That validates our being on this shore
Strangers learning the wondrous mystery of this place
It stands itself. Sacred. Eternal. Always known

INCENSE

Sandalwood smoke shadowless
Slow ascendency, invisible substance
A mirage of being, gossamer sprite

Bearing in its latency shrouded obscurity
Tendril cast skyward in abstraction
Twirling, twisting on unseen currents

Birthing in its insubstantiality
A fragrance of untold, unseen things
Perfume in a fog of imagining

Lifting the spirit to follow its tracing
Out of its nothingness a drifting promise
That powerlessness will bring us peace

Holding us to that which will endure
Even as its cloud-ness disappears
A staircase that carries to enchantment

DANCE MASTER

Was Jesus truly a dance master
As ancient texts say
Teaching others in a whirling cluster
Dancing to the beat of string and wood

Guiding where to place their feet
Which rhythms lead to life
Directing movements light and fleet
On days of Palestinian strife

In step with cosmic lyrics
Dance patterns set since time began
Calling to the lame, the poor, the sick
With me, clap hands as one

A swirl of dancers, tympani
United with the music of the spheres
A magical, transforming company
That cannot be stopped by nails or spears

A RESPONSE TO MARTIN HEIDEGGER IN HIS WORDS

'What lasts in thinking is the way' Martin Heidegger

The wetland seat offers waiting space
That is what it is for
What then are you waiting for
Looking out across calm waters
I am learning in the waiting
What I am waiting for
Learning to understand
The way to what is near
Is the longest and hardest journey
It is the way home to myself
That I wait for
An escape from thoughtlessness
A recovery of centerdness
In an open awareness
That responds to what is given
Coming into a nearness beyond distance
Release from things, openness to mystery
Experiencing enchantment and spontaneity
Where inner necessity is set free
In the disclosure waiting brings
Brief messages from the lost horizon
Of our resolve for truth

REFLECTION

If you ask me about life
I will tell you that time
Escapes into space, like houses where
I lived with loved others, closely watching
For a clue to what was going on
For time is a bewilderment
And space a mooring where
On reflection we can remember
Important things about growing up
Deportment, muscular atrophy, and change
Which comes, spur driven, as the news
Of the death of one as loved as a blood-orange morning
When lifting my head to its wonder
I unexpectedly encountered the Divine
Which untied perplexity's knot
Freeing my spirit to grow

COST

We have been conditioned
To throw too much away
Not because excessive stuff
Because we do not care enough

Issues of import shunned as fake
Of little interest or concern
Politics ignoring needy masses
Circus parades in public sashes

Reducing focus to the shallow
Things that carry little weight
Relieving us of ripened fruit
A facelift cannot hide the truth

When one comes to the narrow pass
Above the chaos of the self
With what to pay the waiting cost
For shadow life long lost

FUNERAL

It did not matter that she believed
At the funeral they sponged
Away all references to her faith
Retelling stories that reflected them

Secular in tone, everywhere implicit
Dismissing in form, omitting in detail
The devout stream that flowed
Deep in her spirit, deep in her soul

A blind indifference to the firm
Foundation she had given them
Turning in their sadness to the shadows
For comfort, unwilling to entertain the light

WEATHERVANE

The weathervane falters
In its time-honoured cockerel form
Arrow above its head alters
Uncertain of the wind's intention
For this generation. Dare I put it plainly
Uncertain of direction

For that is what a weathervane does
Dedicated to pointing the way
Giving intelligence about direction
The North wind on true North at spate
Swinging to the East, West, South
As change and circumstance dictate

No matter what the weather carries
Rain, snow, sleet or warming sun
Content subordinate to direction
A pattern since time began
Assuring travellers and pilgrims alike
This is the way to go as one

This is the direction you must take
Walk in it and I, faithfully, will tell
Of where your future will be found
Your task, your purpose, your goal
For they have little point, each one
If they should lack direction

But now I am confused, uncertain
Ambiguous swirls, buffeted in circles
I turn this way, and that, and turn again
Rattling with perplexity, without assurance
A generation spinning in confusion
Air and spirit seeking lost conviction

What use an arrow if it cannot fly
What purpose a cock that cannot crow
How useless a direction-finder without focus
Spinning like a top in immobile revolution
So I am lost, and you, and all your kin
Who cannot take direction from the wind

WATTLE TREE

I said to the Wattle Tree
Speak to me of God
The Wattle Tree blossomed

So it was
On this clear Spring day
The frothy yellow opulence
Of the Wattle Tree
In joy and celebration
Spoke to me of God

(From an ancient Japanese haiku, anonymous)

COLOURING BOOK

Take the full palette of colours, said Jessup
Creatively make a choice, mixing as you will
Be careful to stay within the lines
Hot colours designated here, others chill

Look at the outcome from a distance
Controlled figure upon a sketched-out page
Confined by heavy border outlines
Unmoving like a vase upon a stage

Turn now to what is all around you
Waving leaves of Winter green, a sparkling brook
Flowing red plains, blue active rolling sea
Nothing within the binding of a book

A constant dance of living colour moving
Enhanced by spectral touches of the light
No constricting edges, patrolled borders
Our colour scheme a form of black and white

Why do we think and act in black and white
Control all outcomes, restrict what we can do
Sadly there is no synchronicity in sight
As if our task to bend life straight and true

DESIGN

All that I do, you know altogether Psalm 139.3.

Iron filing pieces gather in their
Foreordained patterns around
The magnet, centre of their design
Not revealed in its absence

The spring sap runs energetically up
Guided by limbs, branches, twigs
Into an interface of living flowers
When Spring comes by

Water trickles down steep hills
Into streams, amassing strength
Of purpose in river torrents
Directed by pre-existing forms

There is a guiding trace, a line
Forming into a small track
Growing into a path, a by-way
A road, that gives direction

Here is a simple tale, parent of a story
Of short duration, part of a broader
Narrative, opal-veined into saga
Or perhaps myth, where treasure lies

Beneath the randomness, the chance
The ill-disposed splatter, the unfocused
Chaos, there is a ground architecture
Waiting to frame what otherwise seems pointless

TELLING OF ANGELS

The bell comes into voice
Struck from within by a
Directing hammer to speak
Across distances we cannot cross

The gong resonates in deep rootedness
Struck from without by a
Measured stroke, diving, sinking
Into dark places of our interior need

The singing bowl's shimmering song
Born of a moving brush of care
Circles around the chasm of emptiness
Filling aching hearts with sustenance

Sound's reverence, carrying ancient stories
That rise up in us as forgotten memories
Dancing with all we seem to be
Beyond this moment of revery and dreams
Telling of angels

BEGINNINGS

The knock on the door is the primal moment
The opening of the door its culmination
Here is the prototypical beginning
Here starts the dialogue's translation

Is it the moment of God's measurement of us
Or our measurement of the one who calls

Here is a stand-off bringing confrontation
Here is the question over all

To invite the caller in or shut the door
Becomes the action of decision, the crucial gyre
In which all philosophy and religion
Holds its breath, a circumstance powerless and dire

Who is this one stepping across the threshold
Bringing what news, stating a competing will
Here is the doubt, the terror
Here is the gift, the promise that fulfils

The response is decisive, whether understood or not
A moment of whisper thin transparency
Vulnerability stripped bare of all support
An invitation carrying an urgency

This moment bears within trajectories
Directions, tasks, alliances not yet begun
Binding into a whole all that will happen
A new life waiting to be spun

The subject of conversation somewhat obscure
An address sharply defined
After a breath of pausing, reassuring sight
Experience yet to break open, granting light

So the first step
Then another
In the footsteps
Of the other
Do not hurry
Slip or fall
Or call it over

ALL TOGETHER NOW

Jessup lifted his cup. There is a pattern
He said, that cannot be dismissed and should be
Predators oppressing others
Holding for themselves scarce resources
Taking revenge upon those who seek
To overthrow their ruthlessness

A pattern that destroys not only people
But the land itself, viewed as inert, available
Waiting to be exploited by entrepreneurs
With no sense of its innate integrity
Or companionship, essential to sustaining
The life we share on this fragile biosphere

Putting his cup down he looked skyward
There is a crisis coming we cannot avoid
At stake, what we understand the human
To be. It cannot be the case that
Heroic individualism will prevail
We are meant to care and nurture all that is

Together

YELLOW

Bright, brighter, brightest yellow
Comes to its storeyed flowering
Manufactured in cauldrons
Deep in the sun's recesses
Splashed into sun flowers, roses, daisies
Spectacular in tiger eyes
Across sandy beach stretches
Flowing in patterned dresses of young women
Rising out of the darkness
Into another resurrection day
Bringing colour into the essence of life
Joy spilled over the earth forever

FAITH

Living somewhere between faith and doubt
I am sustained by human anticipation
In the very young and wisdom in the very old
Who are not troubled by possession
But resolute in giving and waiting
Beyond trying to pin down the
Profound mystery of our conscious being
Before this present moment of expectation
Whose pulse brings them joy

GOD-CONSCIOUSNESS

How did God-consciousness come to you
Suddenly, as a lightning bolt illuminating
A dark and threatening sky
Gradually, as a realisation that love
Had grown, a small seed into a spreading tree
Or from mother's milk, always there
Deeply indwelling, invisible friend
A sense of presence growing brighter

And did that realisation evoke in you
A life, larger, richer, more satisfying
Filled with a yeasting delight in itself
A sense of more, expanding into newness
Where beauty and joy and possibility
Broke out into a glorious technicolour
Of awareness of otherness everywhere
Was that how God-consciousness came to you

And did it change the world for you
Not just its physicality, but the hidden energies
Moving deeply in all things as sap
Flowing into branch and twig to Spring
Bursting forth in wonder and delight
Where what is the personal you
Named itself afresh and on the way
Was that what God-consciousness gave to you

And did you become freer, more gentle
At ease with silence, at rest in stillness

Able to reach out to others
Without shame, or doubt, or fear
Discovering a deep current of purpose
At work in all you did and contemplated
Finding yourself at home in life's deepest meaning
Was that what God-consciousness gave to you

GOOD FRIDAY

Good Friday dawns again
Cross-hatched with interpretative doctrine
Carrying the freight of years of tradition
As if it might, unexpectantly, be understood

The raw brutality of it remains unchanged
Its sheer facticity as confronting as ever
Compound of nails, spears, wooden spars
Bound by the venality of important people

It does not change but goes on and on
Caught in the retina of the eye, the heart's beat
Everywhere celebrated in ornament and ritual
A roman tree holding up the weight of history

There is no happy ever after
In its cruel unredeemed horror
Always pressing, on and on
No terminus, only the darkness of finality

RESURRECTION MONDAY

Resurrection Monday
No words suffice

Mystery inexplicable
No words suffice

Life overflowing
No words suffice

Joy is the outcome
No words suffice

Resurrection Monday
God's name be praised

BOWLING GREEN

The Bowling Green lies just beyond our back patio
A womb of endeavour producing regularly
Warfare declared among contenders
A game of millimetres, of risky engagement
Driven by the desire to softly kiss
The white porcelain cheeks of the kitty
No lover more seduced, lured into competitive adventure

An occasion of shouted directions, hand-clapping applause
Encouragement, dispute, and triumphant celebration
Muttered curses, ribald comment, hidden anger
And frustration, sometimes beyond bearing

A power drive smashing a winning formation
Raping the kitty with merciless intent
Sending it crashing into the abyss of dark gutters

A time of measuring distances, taking stock
Tactical conversation and shared enjoyment
A constantly renewed endeavour to define
Success and failure, looking for explanation
To explain the deep well of satisfaction
Of each weekly gathering in a context
Where human emotions grow sharp and defined

After, bowls are gently gathered, placed in their
Bassinets, polished to radiant shininess
And put to sleep. The final gathering
For drinks and shared interpretation
Stories and legends beginning to harden
As the day ends, community warmly embraced
The Game counting its money

Standing in the centre of the green in
Darkness, lit by the smiles of thousands and
Thousands of night stars, the gift of time
By light that has travelled countless millennia
To be here. When one looks across
The green there is no remaining imprint of
The human to be seen, only a bare reflective surface

DOVER BEACH REVISITED

The sea of faith once lapped
At Dover shores
Flowing over pebbles
With a melancholy, long retreating roar

The poet, with his love, remembered when
Creation's purposed beauty flowed
Gently around them, then
So various, so beautiful, so new

But now struggle, alarm, flight
Upon a darkling plain
A withdrawing tide from certitude
From peace and help with pain

Faith disappearing like a world of dreams
Here a narrative incomplete, a half-told tale
As the metaphor attests, the tide returns again
A story of the sea that does not fail

   After Dover Beach: Matthew Arnold

SPIRIT

They sing from first floor windows
Guitar and drum and voice
Plague raging in the streets below
Rejoice, they sing, rejoice

Servants of the Pale Horseman
Stalking inns and roads
Long lines of coffins passing
On carts with heavy loads

Above they sing, still joyous
Songs from the people's heart
Singing alone in chorus
United tho' apart

Spirit of the living
Testimony to life
Breaking out of bondage
Defying death and strife

BUDDHA IN THE GARDEN

His vast indifference looks beyond us
Into quiescent dimensions in wisdom's well
Does he care that we have little chance
To reach his undisturbed tranquility

The artifact in the garden niche
Testifies to a wondrous calm
Without outstretched arms or warm flesh
Leaving us on the middle path without enlightenment

He told us the world is what it is
Disappearing beyond it into transcendence
I do not know what I can do
To expedite a meeting with wise absence

DENOUEMENT

You have scattered clues of your self around
Hints, impressions, suggestions, scraps of words
Hieroglyphic enough to puzzle searching reflection
Absent spaces, traces, dropped omens, allusions
A touch of colour, trickling of sand, deep bells
Silent wastes, still mountain slopes, snow covered
Bright Spring daffodils, ripples upon neglected ponds
Times's ambiguity, weighted anchor and winged feet

Sharp edge of water, neglect of air, of trampled earth
Always expectation of another thing, mysteriously
In yes and no of each day's sleight of hand
Suspending certainty when casting away
Questions that hold solutions trapped in ambiguity
Undetected, hidden in the feast, intuition's flight
Where eating together we slip loose, in daring
From time and space, into a moment of meeting
We learn is your denouement

DESCENT

It has been said that the faculty of awe
Is the enemy of intelligence
Which distorts intelligence
And misunderstands awe

Intelligence is not an unconquerable bastion
Teflon coated, of unimpeachable judgment

But a flow of consciousness seeking
To make transparent that which eludes and evades

Awe for its part is an epiphany of arrest
That immobilises our desire to impress
An infolding that is the gift of grace
Which forgives intelligence's success

They are designations of different worlds
Just as setting light makes all trees move
So awe replenishes intelligence so it can
Do its best work, infused by humility and gentleness

YEARNING

The yearning to be loved
Deep in the liquid eyes
Her body slithering across
The antiseptic institutional floor
A grossly deformed lower body
Twisted spine, foreshortened withered legs
Unable at seven to communicate
Except by shouts, grunts, exclamations

These many years later
Her life has long since ended
Multiple images remain
Of that moment in time
One memory does not change
Seeing the hunger to be touched
The yearning to be loved
Deep in the liquid eyes

BRAINSTORM

There is a restlessness of the heart
that pushes at the edge of experience

seeking out the whirring machinery maintaining
momentum, that pulls us along with it

defining small successes, satisfactory outcomes
but never a resolution of the need to reach a further

explanation of imponderable impulses rising out of a
perpetual squall of energy, looking, weaving, asking

delaying, waiting, wondering about the order of things that
seem, despite appearances, to lack a decisive pattern

truly satisfying, leaving untied strings and dragging
commitments never completely dealt with either in

rushes or deliberate stages, since meaning of a
compelling kind remains elusive, hidden from our sight

impossible to trace, weighing the sum total of air and light
hoping all things, believing all things, a river flowing to

an end barely conceived, beyond definition and description
bound by limitations and compelling mystery beyond telling

the endless babbling of a brook, the hum of wires, the
vast blueness of the sky, the silent rise and fall of the sea

that send messages only partially grasped and barely
understood, as present as graves, insistent as bird flocks

lovely as Christmas beetles or fluttering butterflies
pressing us to further exploration, driven by an assembly

of purpose, a network of intuition, that rises with the
morning sun, companion of each day, whispering of

wondrous things, whose provenance apparently is set
at the centre of our existence, always moving, always
promising

set loose by the restlessness of the heart to find
a sanctuary, a pause, a stillness, where love can sing

praising that what is lost is found

GARDEN

Come gently into evening's fall
Pondering a stone rolled away

In the dimness of spread branches
Ask your questions freely

Do not fear rejection
In this still space of acceptance

In this garden shadow
Cast across centuries

Blessing of water will carry you
To understanding its secret

Here where time stands still
Death cannot be found

VERGANGENHEITSAUFARBEITUNG

Despite its luminosity and length
The newly minted German word
Means simply 'working off the past'
A loupe of the mind to magnify
The fissures, cracks and flaws
In history's diamond, cloaked
By propaganda's deceitful settings

Identifying colonial oppression, national destruction
Of the lives of millions, feudal humiliation of the weak
Recognising the refusal to tell the truth of then
Denies us a just and humane present now
Bringing closer to our gaze the truth of what
Cannot be pushed aside or finally forgotten

Both for the oppressor and the oppressed
No national story can be whole
Without repentance for past crimes
And the healing balm of forgiveness
If only English had such a splendid word like
Vergangenheitsaufarbeitung
To help open our eyes and make *us* whole

Vergangenheitsaufarbeitung: reassessing the past/ events in the past.
Re-evaluating events and looking at events which have been overlooked,
shut up, pushed aside or covered up.

DAY'S END

Completing the day by meditation
Accompanied by quiet music
Remembering gracious acceptance
Shared tasks, cups of coffee
A drive through green pastures
Tall trees in afternoon sun
Sharing with old, burnt out men
Disaster writ plain on the T.V. screen
Still the joy of warmth and hope
And things, however small, to do
Turning at last to benediction

God be praised
God's name be praised
God be praised forever

KINGDOM

The Kingdom has come near, said Jesus
In the eating together in peace
Hospitality being the sign of unity
Compassion, welcome, inclusiveness
Wherever hospitality is found
The Kingdom has come near

FULLNESS

Caught in the amber of spirit
Nothing moved
No mouse creep, cicada shuffle, moth wing
All was stillness

The air in the house halted, detained
No sound intruded
As if a moment frozen in time
An eternal now

Ears ached to catch an echo
No resonance was heard
Eyes searched futilely for movement
A dead zone

The presence of ordinary things here
Without attracting notice
Each in its manufactured environment
Proudly uneventful

Clocks arrested, brought to a stop
I too, pinned
Conscious of a profound emptiness
In a timeless moment

An emptiness filled with otherness
That had no visibility
How can one move in stillness
Without destroying it

This was an instance of waiting
Without end
Calling to mind those loved
Without moving

Presented in the unstirred blankness
A world of recollection
As if in the void
All fullness is found

SEMINAR

The Council convened a Seminar
On dealing with ageing
Visiting expert, condescending smile
Lining up his truisms
Shiny with use

Prepare for threats
Falling down stairs
Stumbling on carpets
Slipping or tripping in the gutter

Turning to Jessup
He asked patronisingly
What threats do you fear
The threat in old age, said Jessup
Is well-meaning banality

SPEECHLESS

There is genuine delight
In arriving with nothing more to say
Transported by wonder where words
Are powerless and gone away

Centre in the storm, all stillness
Not needing language to be present
Noise and lightning flashes all around
Moving away. Space without grammar

Escape from subordinate clauses
Signifying inference, metaphoric imagery
Without resonance of the spoken word
Or the soft fall of verbal cadence

Where what is being born
Is a new beginning
Out of the womb
Of the inarticulate

A state of being, understanding
Knowing without speech
The road leads over the hill
A time of thankfulness

Of falling silent, of being free
With nothing more to say
Or needing to be said
Naming the nameless

WORDLESS

There is a violence birthed
By an absence of words
Making it impossible to speak
Of personal pain and the heart's yearning

There is a violence precipitated
By a surfeit of words
That belittle and suffocate
Personal pain and the heart's yearning

There is consternation founded on
Too many words and no words at all
That happens when sharing in prayer
Personal pain and the heart's yearning

There is comfort that arises from
Our inability to penetrate
Inarticulate silence that soothes
Personal pain and the heart's yearning

PROGRESS

Progress is killing us
Like all merciless gods
It requires sacrifice
Destruction and death

Rivers and waterways choked
With plastic and debris
Old growth forests cut down
Beaches stripped mined

Land gouged, poisoned, exhausted
For metals deemed precious
Air polluted beyond breathing
By toxic black clouds and car exhausts

He is beside himself with delight
A new Apple Watch gleaming
Breathlessly declaring its capabilities
I simply wanted to know
How much time we had left

POETIC TASK

If we can for a moment
Lift the veil of life
A brief, bright hesitation
A lightning flash at night

Or open for an instant
A door already closing
A ringing of a telephone
When we are quietly dozing

Then all the toil is worth it
To find words that speak
Impossibly enlightening
The pathways that we seek

The spade deep digging
Deep in the coal black earth
Once again beginning
To find our everlasting worth

HOLY

From whence the Holy
The sacred infused with otherness

From Heaven

That realm no longer claims us
Or fashions by its touch

From Earth

Evolving creatures struggling to comprehend
Compelled to ask, Why is it so? before it ends

If from the numinous

A source not in our ken
Spaceless, timeless, beyond when

If from phenomena

Elusive revealing
Terror concealing

Or does the Holy rise from deep within

To throw a shadow on the void
Mirroring what we cannot avoid

A transient species cursed with entropy
Within the Holy confronted by eternity

Lifted from a crippling malaise
By hope, by surprise, by praise

LETTER

Sorry to bring this up
We are having a bad time of it
Drought, bushfires, covid pandemic
Our bodies are tired, our spirits bereft

To make things worse we live in isolation
Condemned to T.V.s telling of disasters
Bewildered, not knowing what is coming after
We live in consternation

You know these circumstances well
The planet's design included devastation
Was it rushed in preparation
Is this a last round ringing bell

APPARITION

It was a wild sea, a sea without regret
Measured by malice, driven by violence
An imminent threat to small boats

Their boat rose up water mountains, helpless
Plunged to heaving ominous valleys, rudderless
Its very timbers shivering, groaning with trepidation

In the heart of the storm the apparition appeared
Walking on the water, bringing them to terrified despair
Stepping into the boat, coming to them in their deepest fear

WHITE BOARD

White board, immutable, foreboding
Flat, dense white emptiness
Sponged of yesterday's existence
Purpose, desire, passion, hope

Tomorrows clever plans
Designated courses, determined
Aspirations wiped away
A domain without dimensionality

The eye has no focus
The ear hears no sound
No fragrance, no taste
No touching of the mind

Spaceless, timeless, featureless annulment
Without pulse, without colour, without warmth
Anagrams of trackless space or blank screens
Pale reflections of this un-being realm

All devoured by emptiness
Lostness whelmed into disappearance
Present-ness beyond vanishing
Silence wrapped in primal stillness

Essence has no transcript in this void
Emptiness without reach
Vacuum without ground
None-ness lacking depth around

A sense of *numinous*
Creeps into the fibre
Of my being

Tremendum, fascinans
Overwhelmingness

There is no movement
In this great sea of absence
Implacable, unmoving. Terror
At all things gone, erased

An eternity of nothingness
Wonder wondering
Before this nothing
That is not nothing

TURNING OVER

How do we know when it is over
When it is over
How do we know it is done
When it is done
How do we discern the final wager
How understand the turn
From skip ahead to lagging elder

How recognise the quiet dismissal
Accepting that the race is run
Stepping aside without denial
Celebrating our time in the sun
Not seeking to hold the disappearing
Not imagining the time has not come
Out of the chrysalis a new appearing
Let the past go to greet what has begun

A NEW TOMORROW

Poetry is the secret voice of time
The whisper that illumines thought's perplexity
Underneath a cacophony of deceitful declarations
In a marketplace where integrity is loudly sold and bought

Soul-spirit in gentle lute and dance
To be found on the margins, near the threatening edge
Sacred in its lifting of the heart
To make commitment, to offer faithful pledge

Across the pond water, no trace, no map
In the vast steppes red stained distress
Our hands cannot hold a sense of duty
When we cannot praise, wait, or confess

A closing of an inner waste, abandoned
Treeless by the chains that cut its veins
Desolate beyond imagination
Thread-bare clouds without a drop of rain

It is in the stillness we find God's realm
Treasure in a field, a pearl, an inn
Waiting to be discovered in the uproar
Buried in the landscape deep within

We await a re-birth of wonder
A decency born out of trust
Light on a hill, a distant city
A new tomorrow without consuming rust

UNDERSTANDING

The God of Abraham, Isaac, and Jacob
Was more than an idea, more than a conjured necessity

The God of Moses addressed him, sharing a name
Companionable encounter terrifying him to his toes

To talk about God is a pastime of philosophers
But without living presence erudition

Does not illumine the Subject of discussion
That sense alone is made real in dialogue

A conversation only metaphors shed light upon
For there is no language for such intimacy that thrives

What subject to subject insures
Talking about is not talking to

Jesus in the garden did not talk to himself
Or to an idea but with a living partner

From whom his life came and to whom it returned
Only in these terms is understanding found

NECESSITY

It is necessity that demands we sleep
And get up seeking quick relief
Hunger forces us to eat
Energy for greater feats
To go to tasks, regular as slaves
Reoccuring cycle of our days
To make the coin, to buy the pork
To get the strength, to go to work
To get the money, so the rhythm runs
Drum beat, tum te tum te tum

We are more than slaves of necessity
Carriers of a spirit beyond passivity
To make, to do, and to become
To polish apples, peel a plum
To plant, to tend, to care, succeed
So does heart music subvert need
Patterns more than they seem
To create, to flower, and to dream
There is within, reflections of glory
We live to tell most wondrous stories

FOREVER

The microbes in sea mud are 100 million years old
But in all that time they did not have a view
Kelp off Shetland island survived 16,000 years
Moved around a little, but not much

The bristlecone pine, called the Methuslah Tree
Has the status of 4,851 years of age
Remains unmoving where it has always been

Keeping an appropriate distance from all else
Making apartness a singularity
Isolating out of necessity and good sense
All this can be granted as organic know-how
But for such mind-numbing time
With little to show for such persistent discipline

To exist for 100 million years without a view
To wash backwards and forwards for 16,000 years
To be thoroughly rooted for 4,851 temporal cycles
What would be the point. The billionaires fearfully
Building elaborate self sustaining bunkers are
No more intelligent than sea mud microbes
Ocean kelp or ancient trees

For in the end what is the sum of it
A gathered commitment to survival, yes
Without vision, without movement, without gain
Holding to the earth with every fibre
In itself the dominant reason to exist
Without vision, without movement, without gain

CONVERSATIONS OF THE LIVING

(In memory of Brian Walsh)

His life, cancer-slain, nearing its end
Not a matter of how or why but when
We sat talking, of turning the last bend
He was at peace, no messages to send

Death cannot kill us
He would say
From this room I greet
Another day

Death is but a guide
Who cannot pass
Beyond the door
Death will not last

And I will enter
With gladness into life
At the dying of the light
Beyond all strife

Why all the fuss
This my appointed time
To enter into joy
Deep peace, sublime

THE GOD EVENT

If God is the source of the idea of God
Then we always have had a knowledge of God
Each child inherits this truth and apprehends it

When we seek to explore this mystery
We are unable to explain its source or substance
We know more than we can tell, knowing little

We could not tell of what we did not know
Nor can we tell of that of which we do know
Immobilised at levels of experience and thought

The contradiction inescapable, God is all we know
And at once, the Other who escapes assured explication
Leaving us lost for words. If found, unusable

Knowing God then seems impossible
Not knowing God a state of similar kind
Escaping sense and logic equally

Except for that intuition which guides our way
That warmth of heart, a testament to fire
That path before our feet, that goal, that end called love

PHYSICS

At school I did not warm to physics
Despite its generous canvas
Gravity, magnetism, electricity, sound
Heat, radio-activity, air pressure, what to stress
Mysterious forces all around
That sustain our life without distress

Physics, I decided, is the stage
But not the play
Effects, props, moving parts
Background wheels, overlay
Contributing in fits and starts
But not the passion or the rage

Physics is about the how
But not the why that sings
Not the plot, drama or saga
Carrying no climax when the bell rings
Nothing of comedy, tragedy, or saying sorry
Always without meaning's story

It is the limitation of physicality
It cannot touch things of the heart
Or speak in accents to the soul
Provide impulse for a fresh start
Or build a heritage that we inherit
The generous largesse of spirit

SOVEREIGNTY

What day is it, she said
Revealing an inattention to time
Time passing, time shaped by culture's agendas
Laying out weekend tasks, Monday expectations

Each day is like another, she said
Confessing a falling away of responsibilities
Each no longer had sharp claws to snare
Her attention or to demand obedient service

How quickly time goes, she said
Seeing Spring creep up on Winter's end
Admitting her focus was now distracted
Differentiation in the day escaping her

How free it is not to bother, she said
With requirements of no virtue or point
To wear a robe to midmorning and
Shower late because you can

To be free she said, is to kick time in the bum
To make space for doing treasured things
Signing cards, unpicking jumpers, shredding lettuce
Being old is being reborn to sovereignty, she said

ARE YOU READY FOR FIRE?

Are you ready for fire?
The question brought to mind distorted raging skies
Fierce winds, black smoke, burning country roads
Fire, banshee-like, consuming forests
wantonly

Are you ready for fire?
Glowing yellow red in the fireplace
The soft warm embrace of welcome
At the end of a hard day
restoring

Are you ready for fire?
That inner conflagration racing through the bones
Intense conviction flaming to the marrow
Of one's inner being, the mystic's cry of fire, fire
sounding

Are you ready for fire?
Breaking out in community
Flames visible on each members' head
Illuminating spreading contagion
blazing

Are you ready for fire?
Consuming, devouring, nurturing, serving
Gathering into intense centring
Making us heirs of a Phoenix conflagration
gladly

A NEW CREATION

If we had done it
We would do better than God
Banishing the blight of age
Suffering diminished and odd

Disciplining rampaging winds
Abolishing bushfires and drought
Cyclone and tsunami tamed
Reduction of uncertainty and doubt

Food for the starving millions
Health for the sick and poor
Protection for the ravaged land
Equality the prophets saw

Relationships both strong and true
Community warm, hate unsaid
Sanctuary in music and artistic vision
Life restoring the lost and dead

So it would be if we did it
Unfettered joy without pretend
Delighted with our problem-solving
No clearer our meaning's end

END

This is the notebook's end
Pages filled with countless poems
To whom then should we send
These thoughts of opaque omens

Truth is poems have wings
Directions to unknown places
Travelling as the kookaburra sings
Finding rest in waiting places

I wish them well these fairie creatures
Whose passing I record
Compound of thoughts and features
Unique, and yet of one accord

www.ingramcontent.com/pod-product-compliance
Lightning Source LLC
Chambersburg PA
CBHW011317080526
44588CB00020B/2740